Dedications and Readings for Church Events

Dedications and Readings for Church Events

Manfred Holck, Jr.,
Compiler

 **BAKER BOOK HOUSE**
Grand Rapids, Michigan 49516

Contents

About This Book

All of the special services reprinted in this book first appeared in the "Handbook of Dedications" section of an annual planning issue of *The Clergy Journal*. The material, therefore, is tried and tested and has all been used in a local congregation. Acknowledgment of the source follows each of these special services.

None of these services has been reprinted in any other book of litanies, dedications, or prayers. Readers familiar with my previous collection of dedication services, *Dedication Services for Every Occasion* (Valley Forge: Judson Press), will find in this collection entirely new and different services with no duplication.

You may use and/or adapt these materials in any way you wish. They are published for use by local church leaders, and no further permission is required from the publisher or author for photocopying or reprinting provided copies are limited to congregational use.

If a service you need is not listed in the contents, please check the listing in the appendix for many more services available from the author. A photocopy of any one of these other services from *The Clergy Journal* "Handbook of Dedications" is available. Please send $3.50 for each service. Include your self-addressed stamped envelope and the title of the desired service. Send your request to Church Management, Inc., P. O. Box 162527, Austin, TX 78716.

I am grateful to the many ministers who have contributed to this volume. Their willingness to submit their special services for publication in *The Clergy Journal* during the past several years now makes republication of these services available to other busy parish pastors.

There are many special events in the life of every congregation. For most of these events pastors appreciate resources such as those in this book to provide basic guides to the litany or dedication finally adapted. It is my hope that this volume will be useful to you as a resource to help you and your congregation to celebrate the important events in your ministry that deal with church buildings and furnishings and commissioning the people who serve the Lord in special ways.

Thank you for your interest and for your ministry.

Manfred Holck, Jr.

Part **1** **Church Buildings and Grounds**

Litany for Breaking Ground for a Church Education Wing

MINISTER: For the men and women who organized this church in the pioneer days of this community and guided its destiny through those early and difficult years,

PEOPLE: We express our heartfelt thanks, O God.

MINISTER: For all those in the past who were responsible for planning and providing the first house of worship on another location, and then our present church where we are now,

PEOPLE: We express our heartfelt thanks, O God.

MINISTER: For all those present here, and all other members of our church family who are away or have been taken by death, who have thought and planned and given of themselves for this worthy project,

PEOPLE: We express our heartfelt thanks, O God.

MINISTER: For the many who have labored in the raising of funds, and for all who have given with generosity and cheerfulness,

PEOPLE: We express our heartfelt thanks, O God.

MINISTER: For those who have designed the future structure, and all by whose hands and skill and toil the building will be completed,

PEOPLE: We express our heartfelt thanks, O God.

MINISTER: So that the building to be erected here will provide a place of beauty in which our children can learn more about Jesus and his life,

PEOPLE: We ask your blessing upon it, dear Lord.

MINISTER: So that the building may give our children's teachers an adequate place in which to work,

PEOPLE: We ask your blessing upon it, dear Lord.

MINISTER: And from these moments of gratitude and blessing we are led into moments of renewed dedication. To its use for the sacred purpose for which it is now set aside

PEOPLE: We dedicate this ground, our heavenly Father.

MINISTER: And finally, our highest hopes and fondest dreams for the future of our church and our lives

PEOPLE: We dedicate unto you, our heavenly Father. Amen.

INVOCATION: Heavenly Father, we invoke your blessing on us as we meet for this service of dedication. May your Spirit guide us, and may we experience your presence as we seek to prepare ourselves for our spiritual ministry. Grant our prayer in Jesus' name. Amen.

First Congregational Church,
Grand Blanc, Michigan,
Donald A. Wenstrom, pastor

Litany for Sanctuary Being Vacated

(Building destroyed by a tornado)

MINISTER: We lift our voices in praise for the love of God, which we know in the beauty of creation and which makes the earth and the universe to be placed in the hands of people, his stewards.

PEOPLE: We praise your name, O God.

MINISTER: For the pastors and prophets of the past who led the people of God,

PEOPLE: We praise your name, O God.

MINISTER: For the sacred gifts of life, meaning, and eternity, which have been given through our Lord Jesus Christ who lives and gives us life,

PEOPLE: We accept your presence, O Christ.

MINISTER: For the faithful men and women throughout the past who founded and sustained congregations around the world; and for those of this congregation, both in the present and the past, who through dedication to Christ have given of their lives to maintain the ministry and education of the church,

PEOPLE: We love you in faith, O Christ.

MINISTER: For the good years of growth and service furnished by this building; for the love of family, marriages, funerals, sacraments of baptism and Holy Communion, worship, times of healing; for the power of renewal that has been experienced here; for the love experienced in both joy and sorrow,

PEOPLE: We live in your love, O Christ.

MINISTER: We dedicate ourselves

ALL: To continue our loyalty not to buildings but to the church of your faithful people.

MINISTER: We dedicate ourselves

ALL: To continue to build your sacred church on the faith and dedication of our forefathers and to continue to live and maintain the investments of love made here.

PEOPLE: We dedicate ourselves

ALL: To a future of mutually building our love for one another; to doing all things through Christ that his will may be known in this community and all around the world; and to you, our God, we dedicate ourselves.

ALL: The Lord's Prayer

Bethlehem Lutheran Church,
Elgin, Texas,
Al Hoerig, pastor

Litany for Rededication of a Church Building

MINISTER: Dearly beloved, we gather here today to rededicate this church building and its congregation to the purpose of spreading the Word of God. We have expanded our horizons over the past two hundred years; now we enlarge this vision for the years ahead. To do this we rededicate ourselves to the work of God and remember that this congregation with its church building stands as a beacon of light in a world in need of knowing God's love. The church is of God, and will be preserved to the end of time as a fellowship of believers who gather for worship, the administration of his Word and sacraments, the maintenance of Christian fellowship and discipleship, and the growth of believers.

It is God's Word that continues to direct us. Hear his Word as it is written in Jeremiah 32:37–41. (Minister reads Scripture passage.)

Let us give thanks to God for his mercies bestowed upon this church building and congregation, and for his mercies for the future.

PEOPLE: For this place of worship to give God honor and glory; for a place to learn, teach, and

17

serve the Lord; for a place and community in which to witness about the faith and life which has been given to us through Jesus Christ—we give God all the glory and praise due his name.

MINISTER: For all the servants past and present who have led this congregation; for the Word preached, the sacraments administered, the songs sung and music played; for all that is worship we need to give thanks.

PEOPLE: Thanks be to God who provides a place for worship. In worship we are sent to show the good news of God's love to all people by our life examples.

MINISTER: God will provide for the faithful. He provided the means to remodel and enhance the beauty of this place of worship. From the inside to the outside, we rededicate this building for the worship, fellowship, learning, and events to God and to all his people who would enter these doors.

PEOPLE: We truly are blessed in special ways. We do rededicate this building to the glory of God. But just as important, we give ourselves anew as servants of God to provide for others the blessings they seek, for we are examples of God's great love.

MINISTER: You have rededicated the building for the worship of God, and have renewed yourselves to be his servants. Through God we can be blessed by placing our trust in him. The faith of his followers will give guidance to this congregation in the years ahead, as God gives us a new vision of service.

PEOPLE: We accept this challenge and will do what we can in keeping the faith and in sharing God's love with all people and in all times of need.

MINISTER: Therefore, I declare this church building rededicated to the service and glory of God, for the proclamation of the gospel and the service of all humankind.

PEOPLE: Let us rejoice and be glad for the new commitment of service that we have set forth for ourselves this day. With God's help we will so accomplish this goal to be his workers in this part of his kingdom.

MINISTER: Hear the Word of God as it is written in 2 Peter 1:3–10. (Minister reads Scripture passage.)

ALL: The Lord's Prayer

MINISTER: The Benediction

Wampum United Methodist Church,
Wampum, Pennsylvania,
George R. Donnelly, pastor

Litany for the Dedication of a New Roof

MINISTER: Dear friends in Christ, it is our privilege to dedicate the new roof of our building, and ourselves, to God and his glory. "I was glad when they said to me, 'Let us go to the house of the LORD.'

PEOPLE: "Peace be within your walls, and security within your towers!

MINISTER: "For my brethren and my companions' sake I will say, 'Peace be within you!'

PEOPLE: "For the sake of the house of the LORD our God, I will seek your good" (Ps.122:1,7–9).

MINISTER: "How lovely is thy dwelling place, O LORD of hosts!

PEOPLE: "My soul longs, yea, faints for the courts of the LORD; my heart and flesh sing for joy to the living God."

MINISTER: "Blessed are those who dwell in thy house, ever singing thy praise!

PEOPLE: "For a day in thy courts is better than a thousand elsewhere. I would rather be a doorkeeper in the house of my God than dwell in the tents of wickedness" (Ps. 84:1, 2, 4, 10).

MINISTER: Our ancestors built this house of worship for us, as well as for themselves. They saw into the future to children yet unborn, and to those not yet born of God. They were interested in your glory and honor, O Lord, your kingdom, and the salvation of generations born and yet to be born. So we have built this roof for ourselves, yes, but also for your glory and honor and work in the lives of people, and for those who are not yet known to be your children.

PEOPLE: Jesus said to his disciples, "My food is to do the will of him who sent me, and to accomplish his work.

MINISTER: "Do you not say, 'There are yet four months, then comes the harvest?'

PEOPLE: "I tell you, lift up your eyes, and see how the fields are already white for harvest" (John 4:34, 35).

MINISTER: "Abide in me, and I in you. As the branch cannot bear fruit by itself, unless it abides in the vine, neither can you, unless you abide in me.

PEOPLE: "By this my Father is glorified, that you bear much fruit, and so prove to be my disciples" (John 15: 4, 8).

MINISTER (prays): Blessed are you, O Lord our God, king of the universe. The heavens and the earth cannot contain you, yet you are willing to make your home in human hearts. We are the temples of your presence, and this building is a house of your church.

Accept us and this roof and this place, to which we come to be part of the covenant you make through holy baptism, to praise your name, to receive your forgiveness, to hear your Word, and to be nourished by the body and blood of your Son. Be present always to guide and illuminate your people.

And now, O God, visit us with your mercy and blessing as we dedicate this roof and this house and our bodies and our minds to your glory and honor and to the service of all people in the name of the Father, and of the Son, and of the Holy Spirit. Amen.*

Let us bless the Lord.

PEOPLE: Thanks be to God.

*(Prayer adapted from Occasional Services, Lutheran Book of Worship.)

St. Paul's Lutheran Church,
Shelbyville, Illinois,
Robert E. Crofton, pastor

Litany for the Dedication of a Cross for Children's Church

(Begin with a hymn and reading in unison Psalm 23.)

MINISTER: Today we accept the gift of this cross. It is a fitting and thoughtful memorial. This cross will be used on the children's altar to remind our children that Christ died and rose again for each of them. This cross will be a reminder of God's love of his people and of their love for each other within this congregation. We accept this gift with gratitude to those who have given it.

ALL: God of life and Lord of death, we come now before you to remember our friend, to dedicate this cross to that memory, and to dedicate ourselves anew to your Son who died for us.

MINISTER: We dedicate this cross as a symbol of faith.

PEOPLE: We dedicate this cross as a symbol of hope.

MINISTER: We dedicate this cross as a symbol of love.

ALL: We dedicate this cross to the glory of God and in loving memory of our friend, now and forever. Amen.

MINISTER (prays this prayer of dedication): Lord God, we thank you for all of your children who have lived this life in faith and now live eternally with you. Especially we thank you for this day and this moment when our faith and hope are renewed through the symbol of this cross.

We thank you for your hands that created us. Bless the hands that made this cross and bless all of us as we dedicate this memorial gift to our friends. May we always remember that your Son died and rose for us and that it will be the same for those who trust in him, that we shall not perish but have everlasting life.

May the grace of our Lord Jesus Christ and the love of God the Father and the fellowship of the Holy Spirit be with us all. Amen.

ALL: Jesus said, "Let the children come to me, and do not hinder them; for to such belongs the kingdom of heaven" (Matt. 19:14).

The Reverend William R. Daniels

Litany for the Dedication of a Site Development and Parking Lot

BOARD CHAIRPERSON: Having been prospered by our God, and enabled by his grace and power to purchase this land and to develop this site for a beautifully landscaped courtyard area and parking lot,

PEOPLE: We dedicate this site to you, O God.

PLANNING CHAIRPERSON: Recognizing our humanity we affirm our reliance upon God for wisdom and strength, conscious of the faith, sacrifices, and love expressed that have made this project possible,

PEOPLE: We dedicate this site to you, O God. We give thanks for the architect's vision and the labor of those artisans who turned the plan into reality.

CAPITAL CAMPAIGN CHAIRPERSON: We are grateful for those who have committed part of their resources to the capital campaign over their commitment to the ongoing program of this congregation.

PEOPLE: We dedicate this site, this parking area, this courtyard, this landscaping to the glory of God the Father, from whom comes every good and perfect gift; to the honor of Jesus Christ, our Lord and Savior; to the praise of the Holy Spirit, source of light and life; and to the work of the whole church.

First Christian Church,
Frankfurt, Kentucky,
Donald A. Nunnelly, pastor

Litany for the Placing of a Cornerstone

MINISTER: Let "the Temple in Jerusalem be rebuilt as a place where sacrifices are made and offerings are burned" (Ezra 6:3). "The Sovereign LORD says: 'I am placing in Zion a foundation that is firm and strong. In it I am putting a solid cornerstone on which are written the words, "Faith that is firm is also patient"'" (Isa. 28:16). "This was done by the LORD; what a wonderful sight it is! This is the day of the LORD's victory; let us be happy, let us celebrate" (Ps. 118:23–24)!

PEOPLE: As we set this cornerstone, O God, we are building your house in this community.

MINISTER: "You, Lord, in the beginning created the earth, and with your own hands you made the heavens. They will disappear, but you will remain; they will all wear out like clothes. You will fold them up like a coat, and they will be changed like clothes. But you are always the same, and your life never ends" (Heb. 1:10–12). "The solid foundation that God has laid cannot be shaken; and on it are written these words: 'The Lord knows those who are his' and 'Whoever says that he belongs to the Lord must turn away from wrongdoing'" (2 Tim. 2:19).

PEOPLE: As we set this foundation stone, O God, we are building your house to stand for the ages.

MINISTER: "What is man, that you think of him; mere man, that you care for him? Yet you made him inferior only to yourself; you crowned him with glory and honor" (Ps. 8:4–5). "But you are the chosen race, the King's priests, the holy nation, God's own people, chosen to proclaim the wonderful acts of God, who called you out of darkness into his own marvelous light" (1 Peter 2:9). "So then, you Gentiles are not foreigners or strangers any longer; you are now fellow citizens with God's people and members of the family of God. You, too, are built upon the foundation laid by the apostles and prophets, the cornerstone being Christ Jesus himself. He is the one who holds the whole building together and makes it grow into a sacred temple dedicated to the Lord. In union with him you too are being built together with all the others into a place where God lives through his Spirit" (Eph. 2:19–22).

PEOPLE: As we set this cornerstone, O God, we are building your house to serve your church.

MINISTER: "For we are partners working together for God, and you are God's field. You are also God's building. Using the gift that God gave me, I did the work of an expert builder and laid the foundation, and another man is building on it. But each one must be careful how he builds. For God has already placed Jesus Christ as the one and only foundation, and no other foundation can be laid" (1 Cor. 3:9–11).

"Jesus is the one of whom the scripture says, 'The stone that you the builders despised turned out to be the most important of all.' Salvation is to be found through him alone; in all the world there is no one else whom God has given who can save us" (Acts 4:11–12). "For this reason God raised him to the highest place above and gave him the name that is greater than any other name. And so, in honor of the name of Jesus all beings in heaven, on earth, and in the world below will fall on their knees" (Phil. 2:9–11).

PEOPLE: As we set this foundation stone, O God, we are building your house to proclaim Jesus your Son.

MINISTER: "Jesus said to them, 'Haven't you ever read what the Scriptures say? "The stone which the builders rejected as worthless turned out to be the most important of all. This was done by the Lord; what a wonderful sight it is"'" (Matt. 21:42). "Come to the Lord, the living stone rejected by man as worthless but chosen by God as valuable. Come as living stones, and let yourselves be used in building the spiritual temple, where you will serve as holy priests to offer spiritual and acceptable sacrifices to God through Jesus Christ. For the scripture says, 'I chose a valuable stone, which I am placing as the cornerstone in Zion; and whoever believes in him will never be disappointed.' This stone is of great value for you that believe; but for those who do not believe: 'The stone which the builders rejected as worthless turned out to be the most important of all'" (1 Peter 2:4–7).

PEOPLE: As we set this cornerstone, O God, we are building your house in this community, to stand for the ages, to serve the church, to proclaim Jesus your Son, to the glory of God the Father.

ALL: "If the LORD does not build the house, the work of the builders is useless" (Ps.127:1).

Scripture passages taken from Good News Bible, © American Bible Society 1966, 1971, 1976.

Oakland Baptist Church,
King George, Virginia,
Guy D. Mattox, Jr., pastor

Service for the Dedication of a New Sanctuary

We Gather in Praise and Adoration

Carillon hymns of praise with processional

Minister (reads): 1 Kings 8:1–5

Procession with worship appointments:
  Baptismal bowl
  Bread tray
  Wine tray
  Communion linen
  Missal stand
  Lectionary Bible
  Hymnal, pew Bible, responsive reading book
  Offering plates
  Guest book
  Candle holders and candles
  Candle lighter

Chimes of praise

Organ prelude

Processional hymn (choir): "Christ, Thou Art the Sure Foundation"

Salutation; pastoral invocation; "Lord's Prayer," Malotte, sung by congregation and choir

We Offer Expressions of Faith

Choir anthem: "This Is the House that the Lord Has Built"

Acceptance of the new building

MINISTER (reads): 2 Chronicles 7:4–11

Passing of the keys: contractor representative, architect representative, congregation representative

Congregational act of dedication: responsive reading on the house of God (from Psalm 84 LB)

MINISTER: How lovely is your Temple, O Lord.

PEOPLE: I long, yes, faint with longing to be able to enter your courtyard and come near to the Living God.

MINISTER: Even the sparrows and swallows are welcome to come and nest among your altars and there have their young, O Lord, my King and my God!

PEOPLE: How happy are those who can live in your Temple, singing your praises.

MINISTER: Happy are those who are strong in the Lord, who want above all else to follow your steps.

PEOPLE: When they walk through the Valley of Weeping it will become a place of springs where pools of blessing and refreshment collect after rains!

MINISTER: They will grow constantly in strength, and each of them is invited to meet with the Lord in Zion.

PEOPLE: O Jehovah, God of the heavens, hear my prayer! Listen, God of Israel.

MINISTER: O God, our Defender and our Shield, have mercy on the one you have anointed as your king.

PEOPLE: A single day spent in your Temple is better than a thousand anywhere else! I would rather be a doorman of the Temple of my God than live in palaces of wickedness.

MINISTER: For Jehovah God is our Light and our Protector. He gives us grace and glory. No good thing will he withhold from those who walk along his paths.

PEOPLE: O Lord, blessed are those who trust in you.

ALL: We now, the members and friends of this congregation, mindful of the inheritance into which we have entered, and the glorious company, seen and unseen, whose communion we share, do covenant together in this act of dedication, offering ourselves anew to the worship and work of our heavenly Father, through our Lord Jesus Christ. May this hallowed place ever be a haven of refuge, a launching pad for mission, and a symbol of our unity in the faith. Amen.

MINISTER (reads): 2 Chronicles 7:1–3

Congregational hymn of glory to God: "To God Be the Glory"

Offertory, announcements, offertory response

We Are Called to Continued Dedication

MINISTER (reads): 2 Chronicles 7:12–22

Anthem

Meditation

Service of Holy Communion

Hymn of thanksgiving and dedication: "How Great Thou Art"

Choral benediction, passing of the peace, postlude

Shepherd of the Hills United Church of Christ,
Bechtelsville, Pennsylvania,
Vernon Stoop, pastor

Litany for the Dedication of a Church Tower Bell

MINISTER: The great bronze bell, cast in Holland and now hanging in the belfry, is a gift to the congregation from a member who wishes to remain anonymous. Enough it is for him to express his and his family's gratitude to God through this musical call to prayer and worship each Sunday. It is therefore right and proper that we should dedicate this bell to God and to set it apart for its holy use.

To the glory of God, author of all beauty and goodness, giver of all skill of mind and hand,

PEOPLE: We dedicate this bell.

MINISTER: In faith in our Lord Jesus Christ, who has inspired us to offer in his presence our best in sound,

PEOPLE: We dedicate this bell.

MINISTER: Moved by the Holy Spirit, our guide in the worship of God, our inspiration in praise, our helper in the understanding of truth and beauty, love and service,

35

PEOPLE: We dedicate this bell.

MINISTER: To kindle the flame of devotion, and to call by its ringing voice all who hear to worship the Father in spirit and in truth,

PEOPLE: We dedicate this bell.

ALL: O God, our Father, most holy and most high, we thank you for the donor of this bell. We bless you for sounds that make the heart sing and that cause us to turn to you. Grant that we, and all who follow us, shall by the music of this bell be moved to love you better, to heed your will more eagerly, and to praise you more often. May blessing and glory, wisdom and thanksgiving, honor and power be yours forever and ever. Amen.

(Ringing of the bell)

United Community Church,
Sun City Center, Florida,
Russell C. Archer, pastor

Service for the Dedication of a Tree of Faith

(A service of commitment to the stewardship of our money, time, and abilities. Processional out of sanctuary to where tree will be planted.)

MINISTER: Brothers and sisters in Christ, today we seek God's blessing as we gather with thankfulness to dedicate this tree of faith to the glory of God. All your works praise you, O Lord.

PEOPLE: And your faithful servants bless you.

MINISTER: (reads the Old Testament lesson, Deuteronomy 26:1–11, and the New Testament lesson, 2 Corinthians 9:6–15)

Gracious God, you have created the earth and all living things. Without you we are nothing. Even now as we speak, you provide us the sustenance with which to make our responses.

PEOPLE: Lord, you have been faithful to us.

MINISTER: We were once alienated from you, but you sacrificed your whole being by pouring your blood on Calvary's cross for each one of us.

PEOPLE: Lord, you have been faithful to us.

MINISTER: You want us to share your love with others. You call us to proclaim the Good News.

PEOPLE: Lord, help us to be faithful to you.

MINISTER: We share your love with others through our ministries of witness, worship, Christian education, social service, and loving support. These are channels through which your love reaches us and others.

PEOPLE: Lord, help us to be faithful to you by responding to you with our sacrifices of time and abilities.

MINISTER: You have created us to be faithful and responsible stewards, managers not only of our time and abilities but also of our money, which also is a gift from you. Money represents our frozen time and abilities. It is an extension of ourselves, representing a part of our lives. Help us also to sacrifice that part of our lives to you and the extension of your kingdom. Remind us that money without mission is hopeless and that mission without money is helpless.

PEOPLE: Continue to help us to be faithful to you by worshiping, witnessing, and serving you with our money.

MINISTER: Lord, help us to do this by reminding us every time we see this tree, which is a gift to us of your creation, that you have called us to be faithful stewards of what you have given to us.

PEOPLE: You have called us to be faithful managers of our time, our abilities, and our money so that your love may be shared with others through our church.

MINISTER: Lord, enable us to put you first in our lives as we respond to what you did for us with your life. Help us to do this by the way we use our time, abilities, and money. You have left us with this command: "You shall have no other gods before me."

PEOPLE: Let not our time, abilities, or money become gods of our lives, but let us use them to serve you. Keep us faithful.

MINISTER: We dedicate this tree to be a tree of faith. It will be a symbol of our faithfulness to you. We dedicate this tree of faith to the glory of God and to the extension of the body of Christ on earth.

PEOPLE: Let us never forget why we have planted this tree of faith. Let us tell our children, and they their children, of the Lord's goodness. Let all God's people respond generously to his love with their lives.

MINISTER: As the tree of faith flourishes and grows,

PEOPLE: Enable each of us to grow in our response to God's love.

MINISTER: Where there is no vision, the people perish.

PEOPLE: Let us keep the vision. May we never lose it.

MINISTER: The seed has been planted. Will you nurture it?

PEOPLE: Yes, by putting our faith and trust in God that he will provide us with the human and monetary resources with which to make our response to him.

MINISTER: Faith always comes first.

PEOPLE: Faith makes our response possible.

(The tree of faith is planted.)

MINISTER: Let us bless the Lord.

PEOPLE: Thanks be to God.

Hymn of praise and thanksgiving.

(Recessional back to sanctuary.)

Trinity Lutheran Church,
Versailles, Ohio,
Pentti Maki, pastor

Litany for the Dedication of a Memorial Rose Garden

MINISTER: We dedicate this memorial rose garden in remembrance of a friend, neighbor, care giver, and faithful member of the community and of this church.

"And the LORD God planted a garden in Eden, in the east; and there he put the man whom he had formed. And out of the ground the LORD God made to grow every tree that is pleasant to the sight and good for food, the tree of life also in the midst of the garden, and the tree of the knowledge of good and evil. A river flowed out of Eden to water the garden, and there it divided and became four rivers" (Gen. 2:8–10).

PEOPLE: May this garden always affirm for us that the universe is the creation of the Lord God and that we are God's creation.

MINISTER: "Awake, O north wind, and come, O south wind! Blow upon my garden, let its fragrance be wafted abroad" (Song of Sol. 4:16).

PEOPLE: May this garden always be a place for the Holy Spirit to move and blow among us.

MINISTER: "For the LORD will comfort Zion: he will comfort all her waste places, and will make her wilderness like Eden, her desert like the garden of the LORD; joy and gladness will be found in her, thanksgiving and the voice of song" (Isa. 51:3). "And the LORD will guide you continually, and satisfy your desire with good things, and make your bones strong; and you shall be like a watered garden, like a spring of water, whose waters fail not" (Isa. 58:11).

PEOPLE: May this garden always be a place of renewal and re-creation of joy and thanksgiving.

MINISTER: "For as the earth brings forth its shoots, and as a garden causes what is sown in it to spring up, so the LORD God will cause righteousness and praise to spring forth before all the nations" (Isa. 61:11).

PEOPLE: May this garden always inspire us to look for the workings of the Lord God in our day and place, that righteousness may flourish.

MINISTER (reads): John 18:1–4 and John 19:38–42

PEOPLE: May this garden always lead us to see that in the power of God loss can be turned into gain, betrayal and hatred into life—new life for us as disciples of Jesus, the resurrected Christ, and as children of the almighty, eternal God.

ALL: We dedicate this memorial rose garden in remembrance of a friend, neighbor, care giver, and faithful member of this community and congregation.

First Church of Bethlehem,
Bethlehem, Connecticut,
Marshall E. Linden, pastor

Litany for the Dedication of a New Church Sign

MINISTER: "Mary said, 'My soul magnifies the Lord, and my spirit rejoices in God my Savior . . . for he who is mighty has done great things for me, and holy is his name'" (Luke 1:46, 47, 49).

PEOPLE: Thanks be to God who saves us and brings us salvation.

MINISTER: Jesus said, "These things I have spoken to you, while I am still with you. But the Counselor, the Holy Spirit, whom the Father will send in my name, he will teach you all things, and bring to your remembrance all that I have said to you" (John 14:25, 26).

PEOPLE: Thanks be to God for the Holy Spirit who makes it possible for us to know the name of Jesus.

MINISTER: Jesus took a child and put him by his side and said to them, "Whoever receives this child in my name receives me, and whoever receives me receives him who sent me; for he who is least among you all is the one who is great."

PEOPLE: Thanks be to God for all those who received us in the name of Jesus that we might know his name and worship him.

MINISTER: Jesus said, "All authority in heaven and on earth has been given to me. Go therefore and make disciples of all nations, baptizing them in the name of the Father and of the Son and of the Holy Spirit, teaching them to observe all that I have commanded you; and lo, I am with you always, to the close of the age" (Matt. 28:18–20).

PEOPLE: Thanks be to God for those who built this congregation and this church building, making it possible for the name of Christ to be glorified in this community and in the world.

MINISTER: Thanks be to God for those who carried on that vision through a new sign that boldly proclaims the name of Christ.

PEOPLE: Thanks be to God for people like _____, the members of the committee, and those who designed this sign that truly glorifies the Christ.

MINISTER: Thanks be to God for a faithful congregation that helped to complete the building of the sign. And thanks be to God for all those remembered through the memorials that made the new sign possible.

ALL: Because of their faith and their support of Christ's church in the lives they led, they have been remembered even after death, and we have been strengthened in our knowledge of the love of Jesus Christ. Thanks be to God! Thanks be to God!

First Christian Church,
Windsor, Missouri,
Joe Barone, pastor

Litany for the Razing of a Church Building

MINISTER: We lift our voices in praise for the love of God, which he has shown in the beauty of creation, making the earth and the universe to be placed in our hands.

PEOPLE: We praise your name, O God.

MINISTER: For legions of the prophets of antiquity who led the people of God through the wilderness of life into the temple of dedication, even by the faith of Jesus of Nazareth,

PEOPLE: We praise your name, O God.

MINISTER: For the sacred gifts of life, meaning, and eternity which have been given through our Lord Jesus Christ, who lives and who gives us life,

PEOPLE: We accept your presence, our Christ.

MINISTER: For the faithful men and women through the ages who have founded and sustained churches around the world, and for those of this congregation, both present and past, who through dedication to Christ have given of their lives to maintain the ministry and education of the church,

47

PEOPLE: We love your faithful people, our Christ.

MINISTER: For the good years of growth and service furnished by this place, for the love of family, the holy ordinances, the sacraments of worship, the times of healing; for the power of renewal that has been experienced here; for the love experienced in both joy and sorrow,

PEOPLE: We live by love, our Christ.

MINISTER: We dedicate ourselves

ALL: To continue our loyalty not to this building, soon to be demolished, but to the church, which is your faithful people.

MINISTER: We dedicate ourselves

ALL: To continue to build your sacred church on the faith and dedication of our founders, and to continue to maintain the investments of love made here.

MINISTER: We dedicate ourselves

ALL: To a future of mutually building up one another in love, and to do all things through Christ so that his will shall be known in this community and around the earth. To you, our God, we dedicate ourselves.

Central Christian Church,
Granite City, Illinois,
V. Dennis Rutledge, pastor

Litany for the Dedication of Additional Rooms

MINISTER: New rooms have been added to the church building so the congregation can broaden its services and enlarge its contribution to the life of the church. There are here two meeting rooms, a choir room, a kitchen, a minister's study, and a secretary's office. It is appropriate that these rooms be dedicated at this time.

We gather here to dedicate this new building, its equipment, and its furnishings to the glory of God and to the strengthening of his kingdom in this community. We are grateful for the opportunity to build this addition so the life of our congregation may be enhanced, deepened, and enriched through meetings, social gatherings, educational endeavors, the practice of music for congregational use, and the study of God's Word.

PEOPLE: Therefore, we the members of this congregation, with grateful hearts, dedicate this building to the glory of God and of his Son, Jesus Christ our Lord.

MINISTER: In grateful remembrance of all who have loved and served this church in the past and for those who will serve it in the future,

PEOPLE: We do now, with sincere gratitude, dedicate this building.

MINISTER: In appreciation to all who have given their time, talents, and substance so that it might be erected,

PEOPLE: We do now dedicate this building.

MINISTER: To provide an appropriate place where the minds and hearts of all may quest for truth, beauty, and goodness,

PEOPLE: We dedicate this building.

MINISTER: To the teacher of Galilee, who draws all peoples unto himself for instruction and renewal,

PEOPLE: We dedicate this building.

MINISTER prays this prayer of dedication: Almighty God, fountain of all wisdom, goodness, and love, to the truth that makes us free and to the fellowship of all humble and revered seekers after you; for faith, hope, love, joy, and the communion of all believing souls; to the work of righteousness that brings quietness, peace, and assurance forever; to the service of love that never fails, but believes all things and endures all things; to the helpfulness that lifts human burdens by sharing them; to the following of Jesus by our laboring for the coming of his kingdom in our world— we dedicate this building. Establish the work of our hands, O Lord; yea, the work of our hands you establish. Amen.

United Community Church,
Sun City Center, Florida,
Russell C. Archer, pastor

Part **2** Church Furnishings, Equipment

Litany for the Dedication of a Church Van

MINISTER: O God, our Lord, we thank you for this day, for a day of worship and rest.

PEOPLE: We praise you, O God.

MINISTER: For the church of Jesus Christ, your body on this earth,

PEOPLE: We thank you, O God.

MINISTER: For your call to us to be disciples, to reach others for the gospel, to nurture each other in the faith,

PEOPLE: We praise you, O God.

MINISTER: To fostering more spiritual and numerical growth, to healthy Christian fellowship during trips, to ensuring transportation for all who need to come to worship God in his house,

PEOPLE: We dedicate this church van.

MINISTER: To the opportunity to do Christian mission with others, to transportation to and from spiritual retreats,

PEOPLE: We dedicate this church van.

MINISTER: To the equipping of the saints, to the work of ministry, to the building up of the body of Christ,

ALL: We dedicate this van. And we dedicate ourselves to the advancement of God's kingdom and to the proper use of this vehicle as a means of sharing the Good News. In the name of the Father, and the Son, and the Holy Spirit. Amen.

Morningside Presbyterian Church,
Columbus, Georgia,
Raymond Guterman, pastor

Litany for the Dedication of New Church Pews

MINISTER: Rejoice, and again I say, rejoice!

PEOPLE: Yes, Lord, we do rejoice. We rejoice in you, for you alone can give us true joy.

MINISTER: O give thanks unto the Lord, for he is good.

PEOPLE: Yes, Lord, we come to you with thanksgiving, for all good things come from you.

MINISTER: Bring in your tithes and offerings to the house of the Lord.

PEOPLE: Yes, Lord, we bring them in. Our special offering today is the new pews for your sanctuary.

ALL: Lord God, we dedicate these pews that have been purchased and put in place to beautify and bring comfort to your sanctuary. We all give thanks to those who have given abundantly. We thank you, Lord, for giving abundantly to us. Those whose memories or honor are inscribed on each pew we do remember with grateful hearts, for they kept the faith and helped show us the way. Lord, bless these pews to our use.

MINISTER: Rejoice, and again I say, rejoice!

PEOPLE: Yes, Lord, we rejoice; we rejoice in you. Amen.

Five Points United Methodist Church,
Derby, Pennsylvania

Litany for the Dedication of a Cross and Candlesticks

MINISTER: In deepest appreciation for the life and love of the one who is memorialized by every use of this brass altar ware,

PEOPLE: We accept these gifts as instruments of remembrance.

MINISTER: To invoke a spirit of reverence and devotion in the hearts of those who are gathered here in worship, and to summon us to enter this sanctuary in memory of the sacrifice of our Savior,

PEOPLE: We dedicate this cross as an instrument of worship.

MINISTER: To illuminate and shine on the good news of God's love shown in Jesus Christ, that invites each one,

PEOPLE: We thus dedicate these candlesticks as instruments of witness.

MINISTER: Inasmuch as these gifts symbolically represent the truth of God and the gospel of Jesus

Christ, and will enhance the worship of present and future generations of this church with their beauty and significance,

PEOPLE: We now dedicate this cross and these candlesticks as instruments of love.

ALL (pray this prayer of dedication): God of infinite wisdom, who in the beginning said, "Let there be light," we thank you that you have brought us out of that darkness into the light that shines on the entire world through your Son, Jesus Christ.

From the radiant shine of these gifts to our church, we are called to remember that in the darkness of that Good Friday in the shadow of the cross, the light of eternal life could not be extinguished for long; for indeed, on that resurrection day, the light shined so brightly as to dispel all gloom and doubt of the power and might of Jesus the Christ.

We thank you for these gifts that will call us to worship and praise, that from this place the Word of the Son might go forth to illuminate and shine before all of your creation, to glorify you, our almighty Father in heaven, to whom be all honor and praise, now and forevermore. Amen.

> *First Christian Church,*
> *El Campo, Texas,*
> *Jeffrey T. Moore, pastor*

Litany for the Dedication of New Green Paraments

MINISTER: O Lord, we pray your blessing on these green paraments, symbols of your blessed Trinity —Father, Son, and Holy Spirit.

PEOPLE: In your threefold name, we set them apart for their use in this house of worship.

MINISTER: As the green symbolizes life and vitality, strength and resurrection, we remember the lives of our loved ones in whose names we present these paraments.

PEOPLE: In the hope of resurrection and new life, both for us and for our church, we set these paraments apart for use in this house of worship.

MINISTER: Bless our ministry, our witness to your love, Father, in the name of Jesus Christ, our Lord, ever one with you and the Holy Spirit.

PEOPLE: Amen.

St.Peter's United Church of Christ,
Amherst, Ohio,
James R. Foster, pastor

Service
for the
Dedication of
an Organ

Carillon Music:

Preludio No. 9, Matthias van den Gheyn (1721–1785)

Sarabande (1952), Ronald M. Barnes

Suite no. 3 (1953), Henk Badings

    Preludium, Scherzo, Air, Passacaglia

Organ Prelude:

Passacaglia in D Minor, Dietrich Buxtehude (1637–1707)

Toccata in F Major, S. 540, Johann Sebastian Bach (1685–1750)

Choral Adoration:

"Be Unto Me," William Byrd (1543–1623)

The Processional:

"A Mighty Fortress Is Our God," Martin Luther (1483–1546)

The Prayers of Thankgiving and Remembrance

Choral Anthem: "Sanctus et Benedictus" from *Mass in G Minor*, Ralph Vaughn Williams (1872–1958)

The Scripture Lesson: Psalm 150

The Dedicatory Address

The Litany of Dedication

MINISTER: Praise the Lord, praise God in his holy place. To the glory of God, creator, redeemer, and sustainer, that we may worthily worship our Lord,

PEOPLE: We dedicate this organ, an instrument of praise.

MINISTER: Believing that instruments of sacred music are of God and should be used forever in thanksgiving and praise unto the name of the Lord,

PEOPLE: We dedicate this organ, an instrument of praise.

MINISTER: In gratitude to God for his providential love as manifested so richly in the beauty of this organ and in the majesty of its tones,

PEOPLE: We dedicate this organ, an instrument of praise.

MINISTER: To bear up the melody of psalm and hymn and spiritual song in such ways that all may go forth from this holy place with high resolve to do God's will,

PEOPLE: We dedicate this organ, an instrument of praise.

MINISTER: To kindle the flame of devotion, that all who here assemble may worship you, O God, in spirit and in truth,

PEOPLE: We dedicate this organ, an instrument of praise.

MINISTER: To comfort the sorrowing and cheer the faint, to bring purity and peace into our hearts, and to lead all who hear it in the way of eternal life,

PEOPLE: We dedicate this organ, an instrument of praise.

MINISTER: For all who compose the sounds and harmonies that express the hidden feelings of our souls,

PEOPLE: We give you thanks, O Lord.

MINISTER: For this organ, now set apart for use within your house, for its material components, for those who designed it and built it, and for those who will bring its sounds to life,

PEOPLE: We give you thanks, O Lord.

MINISTER (prays): May it please you, O gracious God, to receive and bless this organ that we now dedicate to you. We thank you for the one in whose memory it is dedicated and for those whose gifts make this moment possible. Let this organ, alone or in concert with other instruments and voices, be to all who worship here a source of joy and inspiration for years to come. Through Jesus Christ our Lord. Amen.

The Presentation of the Organ: Spokesperson for the donors

The Acceptance of the Organ

An Ascription of Praise

*Duke University Chapel,
Durham, North Carolina*

Litany for the Dedication of Pulpit Chairs

MINISTER: One of God's many creations was trees. He made them in different species for the diversified use of people. When the time came to build a house, the lumber was available. In the Old Testatment we are told that there were twenty years "in which Solomon had built the two houses, the house of the LORD, and the king's house, and Hiram, King of Tyre, had supplied Solomon with cedar and cypress timber and gold, as much as he desired" (1 Kings 9:1–2). Builders ever since have had a source for their lumber, as much as desired, and out of that supply has come these pulpit chairs, which we dedicate today in memory of our beloved friend.

We therefore dedicate these chairs to the service of worship in this congregation.

PEOPLE: Accept this dedication, O Lord, and bless our use of it.

MINISTER: From the pulpit chair the minister and other speakers will rise to proclaim the Word of God.

PEOPLE: Accept this dedication, O Lord, and bless our use of it.

MINISTER: From the side pulpit chairs participants in the service will rise to read the Scriptures.

PEOPLE: Accept this dedication, O Lord, and bless our use of it.

MINISTER: From these chairs ministers and others will rise to express inspiration.

PEOPLE: Accept this dedication, O Lord, and bless our use of it.

MINISTER: We see speakers rising from these chairs to express thoughts of brotherhood, social concerns, and the teachings of Jesus Christ, undergirded by the prayers of the congregation. We see that they will be able to lead persons to new insights, spiritual growth, and achievements.

PEOPLE: Accept this dedication, O Lord, and bless our use of it.

ALL (pray): "Lord God of Israel, there is no god like you in heaven above or on earth below! You keep your covenant with your people and show them your love when they live in wholehearted obedience to you." And now you have kept your promises to our friend, your servant (name), and today your words have been fulfilled. And so, Lord God, we pray that even as you bless us we shall continue to remember the love you promised and gave to your servant, our friend. You have promised that those who walk before the Lord will be remembered. May our walk before you be remembered by you as you have remembered our friend. We offer these gifts in (memory/honor) of (him/her) and dedicate these chairs to your glory. Amen.

St.Andrew's United Methodist Church,
Palo Alto, California,
Lester L. Haws, pastor

Litany for the Dedication of Pew Bibles

MINISTER: It is a great pleasure today to dedicate the new pew Bibles in memory of _____. It is a suitable memorial for a person who loved her church the way she did, for as a person's knowledge of the Scriptures deepens, so does that person's love of God.

PEOPLE: The Scriptures are the Word of God and the ultimate rule of our faith and practice.

MINISTER: The Bible is an open book. Under the guidance of the Holy Spirit, all believers may interpret the Scriptures for themselves. That is why we have placed an open Bible on the altar.

PEOPLE: That is why we have Bibles in the pews.

MINISTER: Throughout the ages the Scriptures have done a number of things. Through them:

PEOPLE: The experiences of God's people have been preserved;

MINISTER: The laws of God have been declared;

PEOPLE: The salvation of God has been experienced;

MINISTER: The will of God has been spoken by the prophets;

PEOPLE: The purposes of God have been disclosed;

MINISTER: The person of God has been revealed in Jesus the Christ;

PEOPLE: The love of God has been demonstrated in the life, death, and resurrection of God's Son;

MINISTER: The ways of God have been shown and lived by Jesus of Nazareth.

PEOPLE: We praise the Lord, the God of heaven, for the gift of the Scriptures and the knowledge and wisdom contained therein.

PRESIDING OFFICER: As a symbol of the pew Bibles which we dedicate today, I now place one on the altar. And as a token of our appreciation to the donor of these Bibles, I present a specially inscribed Bible to the family.

MINISTER (prays this dedication prayer): We thank you, Lord God, for the precious gift of the Scriptures through which we may know of your gracious presence in our lives. We thank you for the witness of our friend while she lived among us, and for this memorial in her name. May we always be receptive to learning all that you would teach our minds and hearts of your truth. Bless these pew Bibles, O God. Through them may our faith be deepened and our witness made stronger. For the sake of Jesus Christ, our Lord. Amen.

United Church of Christ in Oakley,
Cincinnati, Ohio,
Robert B. Jencks, pastor

Litany for the Dedication of a Clock

MINISTER: Beloved in Christ, forasmuch as God has put into the hearts of his people to present to our congregation this clock, it is fitting that we should, while gathered in fellowship, dedicate it to God's glory and set it apart for its intended use. To the glory of God who determines the times and the seasons,

PEOPLE: We dedicate this clock.

MINISTER: Recognizing that in the beginning God set the stars in their courses, and the sun and the moon by which we can count the hours and the days,

PEOPLE: We dedicate this clock.

MINISTER: Remembering that our finite lives are lived with the ticking of the clock, but that "from everlasting to everlasting" he is God (Ps. 90:2) and that with him "one day is as a thousand years, and a thousand years as one day" (2 Peter 3:8),

PEOPLE: We dedicate this clock.

MINISTER: Mindful that "for everything there is a season, and a time for every matter under heaven: a time to be born, and a time to die; a time to plant, and a time to pluck up what is planted; a time to break down, and a time to build up; a time to weep, and a time to laugh; a time to mourn, and a time to dance; . . . a time to seek, and a time to lose; . . . a time to keep silence, and a time to speak" (Eccles. 3:1–7); and a time to eat and have fellowship together,

PEOPLE: We dedicate this clock.

MINISTER: In gratitude to God for all the time he has allotted us; and with the request that we may be guided in the wise stewardship of it,

PEOPLE: We dedicate this clock.

MINISTER: In loving memory of _____, who was God's faithful servant,

PEOPLE: We dedicate this clock.

ALL (pray this prayer of dedication): We pray, O God, that you will accept this memorial, which we have now set apart in your name and to your glory. May your blessing rest on those who have made this gift and upon all who will benefit from its use. We give you thanks for your servant in whose memory this clock has been given, and we praise you for our memory of him. We ask this all in the name of Jesus Christ, our Lord. Amen.

First Presbyterian Church,
Fort Scott, Kansas,
Gordon I. Zimmerman, pastor

Litany for the Dedication of a Literature Rack

MINISTER: Whatever was written in former days was written for our instruction, that by steadfastness and by the encouragement of the Scriptures we might have hope. "All scripture is inspired by God and profitable for teaching, for reproof, for correction, and for training in righteousness, that the people of God may be complete, equipped for every good work" (2 Tim. 3:16). Continue in what you have learned and firmly believed—the sacred writings that are able to instruct you for salvation through faith in Christ Jesus.

PEOPLE: We thank you, heavenly Father, with a prayer for guidance in understanding and applying your commands and promises to our daily living.

MINISTER: For Sunday school lesson materials and weekly story leaflets,

PEOPLE: We praise your name, O Christ, as we dedicate ourselves to thoughtful reading thereof.

MINISTER: For our church's magazine with information about our denomination and about your worldwide kingdom,

PEOPLE: We offer thanks, with the prayer that we may become well-informed, useful, church members.

MINISTER: For devotional materials,

PEOPLE: We give thanks, O Holy Spirit, promising to seek a closer fellowship with you through daily meditation and prayer.

MINISTER: For informative and evangelistic leaflets,

PEOPLE: We offer thanks, dear God, dedicating our literature rack to your glory and consecrating ourselves to growth in knowledge, and to sharing important printed materials with our loved ones and neighbors.

Presbyterian Church,
Homeworth, Ohio,
Donald K. McGarrah, pastor

Service for the Acceptance and Dedication of Library Tables, Pew Cushions, and Choir Robes

The Organ Prelude

The Call to Worship

MINISTER: God has sent his Son into our world to bring healing and wholeness to our lives.

PEOPLE: We proclaim we have met the Savior, and he has made us whole.

MINISTER: By his touch he opens our ears to hear his message, and he opens our lips to confess him as Lord.

PEOPLE: May we hear his call to discipleship, and witness with our lips to his saving grace.

ALL: Gracious God, you heal the diseases of our lives caused by our wrongdoing, so that we may respond to your Son as our Savior. Heal the deafness of our souls and loosen our tongues, that we may hear your Word and confess with our lips that Christ is Lord of our lives. In his name, we pray the prayer he taught us:

Lord's Prayer

Processional Hymn of Praise

Prayer of Confession

ALL: We involve ourselves in church activities, Father, and yet there is much of what you say that we never hear. We also have difficulty expressing our faith so others can hear. Forgive us for our inability to hear your messages and to share our faith. Give us understanding of your message and words to confess our faith, that all may truly know Christ is Lord. In his glorious name we pray. Amen.

The Gloria Patri

The Litany of Dedication

Library Tables

MINISTER: The pursuit of knowledge is necessary for all who seek to grow in the Christian faith. Therefore a library is an essential part of any church that would be alive, sensitive, and relevant to the contemporary world. It also becomes the center for educational classes as well as for meetings at which the business of Christ's church is conducted. The family of _____ has desired to dedicate memorial funds for tables to enhance the purposes of the library; to make it conducive to study and provide comfort for meetings.

FAMILY: We would honor and remember _____ by donating tables to the library of this congregation.

CHURCH OFFICER: On behalf of the congregation, I accept this gift.

PEOPLE: We dedicate these library tables in memory of _____ and promise to respect his (her, their) memory in the use for which they are given.

Pew Cushions

MINISTER: Seating furniture in church sanctuaries takes many forms. In some ancient churches there was none, and people stood throughout the worship. In frontier days simple benches provided seating. Time passes, however, and now pews are designed to provide greater comfort for the worshipers of God. It is not that such comfort would make people lax and take their ease; rather, it enables our bodies to be more receptive to the moods of worship. Since _____ was one of those who responded to all phases of worship and delighted in a good story used during the sermon, it is fitting that cushions that improve our satisfaction with our worship be given in his memory.

FAMILY: Using the monies given in his memory, we would have these cushions used in memory of _____and to the glory of God.

CHURCH OFFICER: On behalf of the congregation, I accept this gift.

PEOPLE: We dedicate these pew cushions in the memory of _____ and promise to respect his memory in the use for which they are given.

Choir Robes

MINISTER: The psalmist has said that our worship of God includes singing his praises. Thus it is that choirs are a fundamental part of worship. On them rests the responsibility of praising God through their music and also leading us in singing to the Lord. For years_____ was a member of the choir, and singing the Lord's songs was a prime love. Her family has desired, therefore, to contribute memorial monies for the gift of new choir robes.

FAMILY: In memory of _____ and her contributions to our singing the Lord's songs, we donate these robes.

CHURCH OFFICER: On behalf of the congregation I accept this gift.

PEOPLE: We dedicate these choir robes in the memory of _____, trusting they will be worn with pride and honor.

ALL: Almighty God, our heavenly Father, without whom no words or works of ours have meaning, but who accepts the gift of our hands as tokens of our devotion, grant your blessing upon us as we dedicate these gifts to your glory. May these memorials be an enduring witness of the faithful service of those in whose memories they are given. We consecrate our lives to serving you. In Christ's name we pray. Amen.

New Testament Scripture

An Anthem

The Call to Prayer

Pastoral Prayer

Sermon Hymn

Sermon

Offering, Doxology, Offertory Prayer

Hymn, Benediction, Organ Postlude

First Congregational United Church of Christ,
Everett, Washington,
William C. Wright, pastor

Litany for the Dedication of a Hearing Assist System

MINISTER: "My soul makes its boasts in the LORD; let the afflicted hear and be glad" (Ps. 34:2).

PEOPLE: "Let me hear what God the Lord will speak, for he will speak peace to his people, to his saints, to those who turn to him in their hearts" (Ps. 85:8).

MINISTER: In the name of the God of Moses, who directed him to "Gather the people to me, that I may let them hear my words . . . and that they may teach their children so" (Deut. 4:10);

PEOPLE: We dedicate this hearing assist system.

MINISTER: In the name of the God of Isaiah, who foretold, "In that day the deaf shall hear the words of a book" (Isa. 29:18);

PEOPLE: In the name of the God of Jeremiah, who spoke out, "Hear the words of this covenant and do them" (Jer. 11:6);

MINISTER: In the name of Jesus the Christ, who tells us, "What you hear whispered, proclaim upon the housetops" (Matt. 10:27);

PEOPLE: And who tells us of the seed "sown upon the good soil [which is like] the ones who hear the word and accept it and bear fruit, thirtyfold and sixtyfold and a hundredfold" (Mark 4:20);

ALL: We dedicate this aid to the hearing of God's Word, in loving memory of _____, neighbors, friends, and faithful members of this congregation. We give you our thanks, almighty God, for the lives of _____. We give you thanks also that in their memory we are now able to help the hearing impaired hear to their joy, to the strengthening of the church, and to the glory of God. Bless those who are limited in their ability to hear, so that when they come into this house they can know your presence and hear your word and give you praise with all your people. Amen! Amen!

First United Church of Christ,
Bethlehem, Connecticut,
Marshall E. Linden, pastor

Litany for the Dedication of a Sound System

ALL: O God, we thank you

MINISTER: For your acts of self-disclosure and self-communication through the mighty acts of creation, the graciousness of your continuing providence, and the many evidences of your handiwork in the natural world.

ALL: O God, we thank you.

MINISTER: For your Word that you send to all who have ears to hear; through the prophets and priests of old, down through the corridors of time, and into ages yet to come.

ALL: O God, we thank you.

MINISTER: For your message incarnate in Jesus Christ, who in human form gave us a living example of life lived at its best and touched with the eternal.

ALL: O God, we thank you.

MINISTER: For your challenge, responsibility, and command to direct our best efforts toward communicating the whole truth of your will and way to all persons everywhere, beginning where we are, even to the farthest reaches of human habitation.

ALL: O God, we thank you.

MINISTER: For imaginative, inventive minds that devise the electronic technology to aid in the task of communications, as well as for the hands that have labored in the manufacture of the components.

ALL: O God, we thank you.

MINISTER: For all who have purposed to place this sound system for use in this sanctuary and have worked hard to make it possible, as well as for those whose hands made the installations.

Let us pray. Almighty God, by whose work and power all things are made, and without whose blessings we cannot worthily bring anything into the service of your praise, send down your Holy Spirit, we pray you, and let this sound system be dedicated and hallowed to your greater glory, through Jesus Christ our Lord.

ALL: Amen.

St. John's United Church of Christ,
Northampton, Pennsylvania,
Richard Ruckenbrod, pastor

Litany for the Dedication of a Church Library

MINISTER: In the name of God the Father almighty, and in the presence of this congregation, we now dedicate this new library to the glory of God. We dedicate this library to the service of little children,

PEOPLE: That their minds, while young and formative, may learn to live, enjoy, and appreciate the things that are beautiful and true.

MINISTER: We dedicate this library to parents,

PEOPLE: That they may find help in building Christian homes.

MINISTER: We dedicate this library to youth,

PEOPLE: That their enthusiasm may be combined with wisdom and knowledge.

MINISTER: We dedicate this library to the workers and members of the church school,

PEOPLE: That they may have help and guidance to make their work more effective.

MINISTER: We dedicate this library to the leaders of the church,

PEOPLE: That they may find wisdom and knowledge in leading this church forward to ever widening fields of service.

MINISTER: We dedicate this library to all members of this church,

PEOPLE: That we may find here wholesome reading for pleasure and profit and for the continuous development of Christ-like living.

MINISTER: We dedicate this library to our community,

PEOPLE: That it may be a means of service and inspiration.

MINISTER: We dedicate this library to God,

PEOPLE: That it may be a means of continuous service in the building of his kingdom.

Arden Christian Church,
Sacramento, California,
C. Earl Gibbs, pastor

Litany for the Dedication of a Communications Center

MINISTER: God communicates to us through his Word. As we read the Scriptures we see that he spoke to Moses through a burning bush (Exod. 3) and gave the Ten Commandments to Moses on Mt. Sinai (Exod. 20). When our Savior, Jesus Christ, was crucified, a sign was written and placed above his head on the cross for the public to see: "Jesus of Nazareth, the King of the Jews" (John 19:19).

PEOPLE: We see this communications center as a place to share the good news of Jesus Christ and of this congregation.

CHAIRPERSON, OFFICIAL BOARD: May this communications area carry on the business and administration of this congregation through the use of mailboxes for church staff, church officers, and committee members; along with the church calendar for the purpose of keeping an orderly schedule of services, programs, and events in public view for all concerned.

PEOPLE: We see this communications center as a place to share the good news of Jesus Christ and of this congregation.

CHAIRPERSON, TRUSTEES: The bulletin board area of this communications center provides space for the posting of information and announcements of this church from a variety of church groups—Christian Unity, Church and Society, Christian Education, Stewardship and Worship—as well as community and area organizations, so that all who desire to know, serve, and share the love of Jesus Christ more fully every day will be informed.

PEOPLE: We see this communications center as a place to share the good news of Jesus Christ and of this congregation.

CHAIRPERSON, COMMUNICATIONS COMMITTEE: Showing the locations of the missionaries, mission stations, and projects we support on local, national, and world maps will inform us of our call and response "to go into all the world" through our missions' work. Evangelism will be represented by locating all our church members on the local, county, and world maps. The care of our membership, and outreach beyond, will be seen through the use of the marker board listing those persons hospitalized and in nursing homes. Pictures of our newest members, people most recently baptized, and newlyweds will be displayed on the bulletin board.

PEOPLE: We see this communications center as a place to share the good news of Jesus Christ and of this congregation.

CHAIRPERSON, MEMORIALS COMMITTEE: We are happy to have known and been the joyful recipients of the pastoral leadership of our Minister, whose fruitful ministry we recognize through the dedication of this communications center today.

ALL: We dedicate this communications center as a place to share the good news of Jesus Christ and of this congregation.

MINISTER: Let us pray.

ALL: Almighty God, who continues to communicate your word to and through our lives in many forms, times, and places, speak to us anew through this communications center. As you have spoken through your servant, _____ , in whose memory we dedicate this center, continue to speak through us in your wondrous and truthful ways. For we rededicate ourselves to spreading the good news of your Son, Jesus Christ, from this communications center, from your written Word, and by the example of our lives. In the name of the Father, Son, and Holy Spirit we pray. Amen.

Asbury United Methodist Church,
Albion, Indiana,
Joe Andrews, pastor

Part **3** **Church People**

Litany for the Installation of a Director of Christian Education

MINISTER: Today we have the privilege and opportunity of installing _____ as director of Christian education within the life of this congregation. We take these moments to stop and consecrate _____ to this position of leadership in our church family.

_____, do you accept the office to which you have been selected, and do you promise, the Lord being your helper, faithfully to fulfill its duties?

CANDIDATE: I do.

MINISTER: We have the privilege of working together on the staff of this church. Do you pledge your cooperation and good faith to the staff as we also pledge this same support to you?

CANDIDATE: I do.

MINISTER: All people who are involved in Christian education within this congregation, I now ask you to pledge your support as _____ leads and gives direction to this ministry.

CHRISTIAN EDUCATION STAFF: We will.

MINISTER: All who consider this congregation to be your church home, I now ask you to respond together, showing your support of _____ as our director of Christian education. Please stand as an indication of your support. We now join together in the installation prayer.

MINISTER: (prays an installation prayer)

MINISTER: As the pastor of this congregation I now declare _____ to be the director of Christian education with all the rights, privileges, and responsibilities that this office holds. May the Lord Jesus Christ strengthen you for this task.

Brethren in Christ Church,
Carlisle, Pennsylvania,
Kenneth O. Hoke, pastor

Litany for the Farewell to a Family

MINISTER: Our faith can change the lives of people we don't even know. We thank God for the opportunity to have shared a portion of life's journey with this family, and now we send them forth to bring the faith we've mutually strengthened to others we do not know.

PEOPLE: "Now faith is the assurance of things hoped for, the conviction of things not seen. For by it the men of old received divine approval. By faith we understand that the world was created by the word of God, so that what is seen was made out of things which do not appear" (Heb. 11:1–3).

MINISTER: We join the writer of Hebrews in giving thanks for the faith of all who witness to the living God. As the writer thanks God and finds strength in the faith of Abraham, Moses, David, and many others, so do we find strength in the faith and service this family and many others in this place bring to us.

PEOPLE: We thank God for all the ways in which this family and all other faithful witnesses have served, and we acknowledge that we, too, have been witnesses to them.

MINISTER: Apart from Jesus and our fellowship in him, we cannot be made perfect, and so we ask all families to join us in this commitment.

PEOPLE: "Therefore, since we are surrounded by so great a cloud of witnesses, let us also lay aside every weight, and sin which clings so closely, and let us run with perseverance the race that is set before us, looking to Jesus the pioneer and perfecter of our faith, who for the joy that was set before him endured the cross, despising the shame, and is seated at the right hand of the throne of God" (Heb. 12:1–2).

MINISTER: We trust you will go forth and find another loving fellowship in which to witness, taking with you the love, the faith, and the continual welcome of our congregation.

ALL: Amen.

First Christian Church,
Windsor, Missouri,
Joe Barone, pastor

Litany for the Dedication of the Roster of Our Pastors

MINISTER: "Now faith is the assurance of things hoped for, the conviction of things not seen.

PEOPLE: "For by it the men of old received divine approval. By faith we understand that the world was created by the word of God, so that what is seen was made out of things which do not appear" (Heb. 11:1–3).

MINISTER: We stand in covenant with all of God's people of all time;

VOICE 1: With Noah and a sign of the covenant: the rainbow;

VOICE 2: With Abraham and Sarah and a sign of the covenant: a child named laughter;

VOICE 3: With Moses and a sign of the covenant: the two tables of the Ten Commandments;

VOICE 4: And with Ruth and Esther,

VOICE 5: Amos, and Hosea, and Isaiah, and Jeremiah;

MINISTER: With Christ Jesus, and the twelve; with all who have gathered in this house of worship, our congregation, for a quarter of a millennium for the sacrament of the Lord's Supper.

PEOPLE: Today we dedicate this roster of our pastors, recalling their service in the name of the one Lord, Jesus Christ:

VOICE 6: Names famous and names obscure,

VOICE 7: Names ancient and names contemporary,

VOICE 8: Names unknown and names fondly remembered.

MINISTER: Reaffirming the covenant by which we journey, and thanking God for faithful people of our time and all times, we dedicate this roster of our pastors by standing to join together in the covenant of our congregation.
"Therefore, since we are surrounded by so great a cloud of witnesses,

PEOPLE: "Let us also lay aside every weight, and sin which clings so closely, and let us run with perseverance the race that is set before us,

ALL: "Looking to Jesus the pioneer and perfecter of our faith, who for the joy that was set before him endured the cross, despising the shame, and is seated at the right hand of the throne of God" (Heb. 12:1–2). Amen! Amen!

First Church of Bethlehem,
Bethlehem, Connecticut,
Marshall E. Linden, pastor

Litany for the Commissioning of Church School Teachers

MINISTER: Will the following persons—teachers and administrators in our church school—please come forward. (As each teacher is called to the front of the sanctuary, members of his/her class will stand for a moment and then be seated. The names of the teachers should be called slowly enough to add dignity to the service and give the students time to respond.)

Teaching in the church school is a covenant, an agreement between the teacher, God, the parents, the students, and the congregation. In this covenant all parties agree to carry out their respective responsibilities.

Teaching in the church school is one of the most important tasks a member of the church can assume. Being a church school teacher indicates you are committed to the cause of Christ, and you believe in the love of God as revealed through Jesus Christ. There will be hours of preparation, opportunities to share with others the faith you have, and lives changed because you have agreed to be a part of the continuation of Christ's teachings. Will you now recommit yourself to this task?

TEACHERS: I will, the Lord being my helper. I understand and accept the need to work with diligence on the preparation of the lesson materials, to attend worship services as a part of my witness and teaching, and to seek God's guidance.

MINISTER: All church school teachers represent more than only themselves. They represent all other members of the church. Indeed, work that can be accomplished by any church school teacher is either enlarged or limited in direct proportion to the support given by all members of the congregation, including family members of students and teachers.

Members of the congregation, will you commit yourselves to this task, supporting your teachers both in service and in financial resources? Will you pray for the success of your church school, through prayers in the form of actions as well as prayers in the form of words?

Will you entrust the Christian education of this congregation into the hands of these committed teachers and leaders?

PARENTS: We are grateful that these persons agree to be the church school teachers of our children, and we will carry out our responsibilities as also being teachers by such Christian examples as praying in the home, encouraging preparation for church school, and taking part in the weekly worship services.

MEMBERS: We rejoice that these persons will accept the responsibility of teaching in the church school; we promise they will not stand alone. Because they act in our name, and in the name of Christ, we commit ourselves to supporting them as they seek to bring to full flower the Christian understanding and education of those placed in their care. We pray God's blessing on them.

THE SIGN OF THE COVENANT (A rosebud may be presented to each teacher. The bud represents the student whose Christian education will be expanded by the teacher.)

MINISTER: (prays a prayer of commissioning).

United Methodist Church,
Lynden, Washington,
Miles Walter Jackson, pastor

Litany for the Commissioning of a Director of Music

MINISTER: We now set apart and commission our friend and brother/sister in Christ, _____, to the work of director of music, commending him/her by prayer to the grace of God. As your pastor and friend, and on behalf of this congregation, I ask you now to tell us of your call to this task.

Do you believe that you have been called of God to exercise this ministry of praise and education in this congregation?

CANDIDATE: I do.

MINISTER: Do you promise to be faithful in this task, treating those in your care with love and respect, helping them to do their best through example, leading us all to more worthily praise our God and Savior?

CANDIDATE: I do, the Lord being my helper and strength.

MINISTER: And now, so that _____ and each of us understand that this ministry is shared, that the burden is not his/hers, alone, let us all stand and commit ourselves to the ministry of praise in music.

ALL: We promise as your friends in Christ that we will do all we can to make your task fulfilling and joyful. We will make our joyful noise with gusto and enthusiasm. We will respond to your leading with openness. We will examine with interest every activity in which you ask us to take part, and we will join you whenever time and talent allow. Above all, we will remember you are as we are, in need of grace, and so we will pray for you.

MINISTER (prays this prayer of commissioning): O Lord, our God, we ask you to bless your servant _____ to whom the trust has been committed of leading the musical praises of your people within this place. As you have called him/her to your service, make and keep him/her worthy of this calling. Let your Spirit rule and direct his/her heart in all the duties given to him/her, that he/she may teach and lead others to offer their worship in reverence and to sing with understanding and heart to you, and not primarily to those around. And grant that his/her fellowship with this family of faith may be such that together we will continually find joy and growth in this service of praise. Through Jesus Christ our Lord we pray. Amen.

Temple Baptist Church,
Windsor, Ontario, Canada,
William Norman, pastor

Litany for the Installation of Church Officers

(Suggestions for conduct of litany:

1. If officers sit as boards at the front of the sanctuary, they can more easily step out as a group when their board is presented.

2. In the roll call of the officers, the names of officers-elect are called first, and then the continuing officers.

3. When officers' names are called, they turn facing the congregation so that the members will be able to identify them.

4. An appropriate theme might be the importance of volunteerism as a ministry of the church to the life of the community.

5. The statement of faith of the church, Apostles' Creed, or some other affirmation could be used appropriately as a part of the service.)

MINISTER: In the churches of our faith and order, much of the responsibility for the ministry of the congregation is entrusted to the laity. In like manner, this congregation, seeking the guidance of the

Holy Spirit, has chosen persons to serve in their appointed places—to be associated with their fellow members already so serving and with the pastor and other members of this staff. In preparation for their installation, let us hear the instruction of the apostle Paul to all of us. (Minister reads Romans 12:4–8.)

We celebrate our varied gifts of the one Spirit. In their commitment now, may these officers complement one another to build up the body of Christ to the full maturity that was in him.

ALL: Praise be to God for the creativity of his love in the many gifts manifest among us.

MINISTER: Let us give attention to the roll call of the officers and officers-elect: *board members*

OFFICERS-ELECT *and Board members* (stand): Having been nominated by the personnel board and duly elected by the congregation at its annual meeting, we do now present ourselves for installation.

MINISTER: God's call has been sounded through his church. You have been responsive to this call. In these moments you come offering your gifts of personality, talent, energy, and time in ministry *to* through this congregation. May your position of leadership be not just a job to be done but an opportunity to grow in all Christ-like graces; may you celebrate the church in new relationships; may you discover life's meaning in service.

OFFICERS-ELECT *and Board members!*: If there is something I can do, I want to do it wholeheartedly as unto the Lord. I will need the trust, prayers, and encouragement of my fellow officers and fellow members. I now commit myself and the gifts of God's love and grace to me, that with the quickening of his Spirit I may become that instrument of his to which the church is calling me.

MINISTER: Will you officers previously chosen and having served as leaders pledge your cooperation and support to these newly elected officers, that together you may give effective leadership to this congregation?

CONTINUING OFFICERS (stand): We receive these our fellow officers and give ourselves in a renewed sense of loyalty to the ministry in which we serve.

MINISTER: As members of the staff, it is our privilege to work as co-ministers with you who are leaders in the life of this congregation. Our first responsibility is to equip you for ministry. We are here to instruct, to counsel, to support, but not to usurp your ministry.

What response do you, who are members of this congregation make to your fellow members whom you have elected to positions of leadership? If you wish to respond, you may rise, indicating your desire to stand in commitment with them.

PEOPLE (stand): We members of this congregation sense our responsibility to give ourselves in support of the ministry to which you give leadership. "We are members one of another." We are called to minister to each other and to the world. Together we need to discover what God is calling this congregation to be and to do. We need to dream together, study together, worship together, serve together. Together may we exalt Christ, the head of the church. For our ~~ministry~~ *Service* may we experience the light and strength of God's own Spirit.

ALL: Once we were no people, but now we are God's people. Once we had not received mercy, but now we have received mercy, that we may declare the wonderful deeds of him who called us out of darkness into his marvelous light (1 Peter 2:9–10, adapted).

MINISTER (prays this prayer for all church officers): Our heavenly Father, the giver of every good and perfect gift, we rejoice in the gifts that you have given to us: the different talents, the diverse opportunities of education, the varying experiences that life affords. We praise you for the enrichment that comes to the life of the church as these gifts are enthusiastically committed and faithfully exercised. We thank you for these men and women who have answered the call to Christian service through election to leadership responsibilities in this congregation, and who come at this time to dedicate their different gifts to your ~~ministry~~ *Church*.

O Lord, bless those officers who lead this congregation with insight into the truth, love for people, a zeal that never flags, and a strength that comes from a consciousness of your presence. As a congregation may we receive all these officers as servants of yours and give ourselves in loyal support to the program they project in their areas of responsibility. Confronted with demanding responsibilities, we do not ask for lesser tasks but for a faith equal to our tasks. Increase in each of us the ability to receive the fullness of your grace and truth expressed in Jesus Christ. Strengthen us in all things to build on Christ, the chief cornerstone, so that we are as living stones built into a spiritual house.

You care for all people and conditions of people. We lift to you the life that we share as a congregation: heal our infirmities, awaken us to our great opportunity, strengthen our aspirations to serve. Where there is illness in our families, we pray for health. Where there are problems that perplex us, we pray for knowledge of your will and the courage to follow it. Where there is sorrow, either in the present or in remembrance, we pray for the strength of your comfort. Be with those who serve your church in other lands, that theirs may be a faithful witness to your love for all persons. Strengthen the leaders of this nation and all world leaders in their concern for truth, justice, and righteousness. Be with those who risk their lives in bringing the gospel of reconciliation to the troubled areas of our world. For your sake and for the sake of all of those for whom we have responsibility we pray. Amen.

First Congregational Church,
United Church of Christ,
Sarasota, Florida,
John Thompson, pastor

Part **4** **Church
Program**

Litany for the Dedication of a Scholarship Trust Fund

MINISTER: The Lord has been our dwelling place from generation to generation.

PEOPLE: From everlasting to everlasting you are God!

ALL: We will tell to the coming generation the glorious deeds of the Lord, that the next generation might know them, that the children yet unborn may arise and tell them to their children, so that they should set their hope in God.

MINISTER: We are here today to dedicate our gift to future generations of students—the _____ Church Scholarship Trust Fund. By the grace of God and the dedication of God's people in this congregation, we have chosen to share our blessings with our students who seek the wisdom of education, that we might raise up strong leaders for the church and the world. We are conscious that we stand surrounded by a great cloud of witnesses who have gone before us, who have led us in ministry by faithful example in the stewardship of their whole lives. We seek to carry on their example of hope and trust.

113

Many hands have been put to the task of establishing this scholarship trust fund. It is right to recognize their contribution.

PEOPLE: We thank you, eternal God, for the faithfulness and vision of these your servants, and for
their dedication and guidance in establishing our
scholarship trust fund. May the blessings from this
fund far exceed our fondest hopes.

MINISTER: As stewards of the Christian faith, we
are responsible for passing on the love of Jesus Christ
in all of its manifestations. When asked which was
the greatest commandment of all, he answered, "The
first is, 'Hear, O Israel: The Lord our God, the Lord is
one, and you shall love the Lord your God with all
your heart, and with all your soul, and with all your
mind, and with all your strength.' The second is this,
'You shall love your neighbor as yourself.' There is
no other commandment greater than these." With
this scholarship trust fund, you have demonstrated
your love for your neighbors of the future, and your
commitment to training them to love our God with
their whole minds through their pursuit of God's
truth through education.

I now ask you: Do you affirm your love for your
neighbors of future generations?

PEOPLE: The Lord being our help, we do.

MINISTER: Do you pledge yourselves to help them
to learn what it means to love God with their whole
minds?

PEOPLE: The Lord being our help, we do.

MINISTER: As stewards of the Christian faith, will you accept the challenge to shepherd the future leaders of God's church through the scholarships you award?

PEOPLE: The Lord being our help, we will.

MINISTER (prays): Almighty God, the fountain of all wisdom, enlighten by your Holy Spirit those learners who will benefit from this scholarship trust fund, that rejoicing in the knowledge of your truth they may worship you and serve you with all their hearts, all their souls, all their minds, and all their strength. Bless those who, through their love for you, contribute to and oversee this scholarship trust fund, that they may as wise and faithful stewards enter into the joy of their master. Bless, O Lord, this scholarship trust fund, that its light might so shine before all people that they will give glory to you. Amen.

MINISTER: Now to him who by the power at work within us is able to do far more abundantly than all we ask or think, to him be glory in the church and in Christ Jesus to all generations, for ever and ever. Amen.

First Christian Church,
Burnet, Texas,
Robert R. Howard, pastor

Litany for the Renewal of Marriage Vows

MINISTER: We come together today for a very special reason. _____ and _____ desire to renew their marriage vows of faith, love, and fidelity here in the presence of God and of this company. They ask you to be a part of this worship service because it is special to them, a special expression of their love of God and each other.

The Lord be with you.

PEOPLE: And also with you.

MINISTER (prays): Almighty God, we thank you for this day that we celebrate in your name. We ask your blessings on the renewal of marriage vows of _____ and _____ . They know you have been with them over the years, and they seek your continued presence. When they first offered their vows to each other and before you twenty-five years ago, they remembered that your Son Jesus performed his first great work at the marriage in Cana of Galilee.

Help them and us to realize that you continue to be with us today. We ask you to bless them in this endeavor in the name of Jesus Christ, our Lord. Amen.

MINISTER: _____ and _____ , as you stand before God and this company preparing to renew your vows of marriage, you cannot help but be reliving in your minds many of the events of your life together over the last twenty-five years.

When you stood before the altar of Christ to offer your marriage vows for the first time, you were but as children making promises that you did not fully understand. You promised to live together for better or worse, for richer or poorer, in sickness and in health, and you couldn't know exactly what that meant. You made your affirmative response in faith that God would be with you in all times.

Now, twenty-five years later, you know what those promises mean. You know what "in sickness and health" means; you have seen the ups and downs of everyday living; you understand what "richer or poorer" means. You know what it means to experience the high moments of life as well as the low.

Now is a time for you, standing before God and this company, to renew your vows of marriage one to the other. What do you choose to say?

HUSBAND: _____ , I love you as I love no other person. All that I am I share with you. I will continue to be your husband through sickness and health, through joy and sorrow, through poverty and plenty, now and forever. I offer this vow in the name of God the Father, God the Son, and God the Holy Spirit. Amen.

WIFE: _____ , I love you as I love no other person. All that I am I share with you. I will continue to

be your wife through sickness and health, through
joy and sorrow, through poverty and plenty, now
and forever. I offer this vow in the name of God the
Father, God the Son, and God the Holy Spirit.
Amen.

MINISTER: No more fitting or better advice will
come to you than to remind you of that offered by
the apostle Paul when he wrote: "Love is patient
and kind; love is not jealous or boastful; it is not
arrogant or rude. Love does not insist on its own
way; it is not irritable or resentful; it does not
rejoice at wrong, but rejoices in the right. Love bears
all things, believes all things, hopes all things,
endures all things. Love never ends" (1 Cor. 13:4–8).
_____ and _____ , what tokens do you offer
one another as signs of your continuing love and
commitment? (Rings or other tokens are handed to
minister.)
Almighty God, heavenly Father, eternal Spirit, bless
the giving and receiving of these rings. Through the
wearing of these rings may _____ and _____ be
reminded continually of their vows and of your presence in their marriage. In the name of Christ we pray.
Amen. (Rings are handed to couple.)

HUSBAND: _____ , receive and wear this ring as
a reminder of my love for you and a renewal of my
commitment.

WIFE: _____ , receive and wear this ring as a reminder of my love for you and a renewal of my
commitment.

MINISTER: The Lord be with you.

PEOPLE: And also with you.

MINISTER (prays prayer for renewal of marriage vows, followed by Lord's Prayer.)

_____ and _____ , having been privileged to hear these vows of renewal you have made to each other and witnessed by this congregation, it is with joy that I renew the declaration that you are husband and wife together, in the name of the Father, and of the Son, and of the Holy Spirit. Go now in peace, and remember you are the children of God.

PEOPLE: Amen. May the God of love grant you to live in the peace and harmony with each other that will prepare you for life in the world to come, life in God's everlasting love.

MINISTER: Amen. May the blessing of almighty God—Father, Son and Holy Spirit—be with you now and forever.

PEOPLE: Amen. Thanks be to God.

United Methodist Church,
Lynden, Washington,
Miles Walter Jackson, pastor

Service for the Celebration of a Church's Fiftieth Anniversary

Prelude and Processional Hymn

MINISTER: Praise the Lord! Praise the name of the Lord.

PEOPLE: Praise the Lord! Give thanks to him.

MINISTER: He has blessed us and brought us to this time.

PEOPLE: He has blessed us and brought us to this place.

MINISTER: He has caused his name to dwell in our midst.

PEOPLE: He has stirred our hearts and made us glad.

MINISTER: He has shown us his glory in his mighty Word.

120

PEOPLE: He has shown us the way to truth and life.

MINISTER: Praise the Lord! Praise the name of the Lord.

PEOPLE: Praise the Lord! Give thanks to him.

MINISTER: For fifty years he has filled and sustained us.

PEOPLE: For fifty years he has shown us his grace.

MINISTER: For fifty years he has given himself to us in word and sacrament.

PEOPLE: For fifty years he has empowered us with his Holy Spirit.

MINISTER: For fifty years he has given us to be his witnesses to the world.

PEOPLE: For fifty years he has given us to be in loving fellowship with one another.

MINISTER: Praise the Lord forevermore. Oh, praise the name of the Lord.

Hymn of Praise

Salutation

Prayer of the Day

Lessons

Hymn of the Day

Sermon

Hymn

MINISTER: The Lord God in his goodness has blessed us with fifty years of service as _____ Church. We are a remembering people, and it is good that we remember that he has chosen us, and baptized us, and brought us together as a congregation. We are a remembering people, looking back at all the saving acts of God: the creation, the flood, the covenant, the exodus, the incarnation, the crucifixion, the resurrection, the church. We are a remembering people, but we are also a people of this day with an eye to the future. A church is not a building. A church is the fellowship of believers —the body of Christ sharing, caring, working in the world, and living in the hope of the world to come. Therefore, mindful both of our heritage and our vision for the future, let us dedicate ourselves to the care and redemption of all that he has made.

PEOPLE: Almighty God, we give you thanks for the work you have done in this place. We give you thanks for your love and faithfulness. When we called on your name, you made your presence known to us. When we prayed, you heard us. When we preached your Word and administered your sacraments, you were in our midst. You have accepted our humble sacrifices of praise and thanksgiving. You have listened to our confessions and forgiven our sins. And you have sent your Holy Spirit to heal and comfort us in our hurts, our sorrows, our infirmities, and our losses.

MINISTER: Continue to empower us with your Spirit, O Lord, that we might proclaim your gospel to all people.

PEOPLE: We dedicate our lives to your service.

MINISTER: Help us to witness to the good news of Jesus Christ in all that we do and say.

PEOPLE: We dedicate our lives to your service.

MINISTER: Show us how we might give care and support to the needy, and love and mercy to the broken and forlorn.

PEOPLE: We dedicate our lives to your service.

MINISTER: Show us that arms are for loving, and that loving is for fellow believers and for all those around us.

PEOPLE: We dedicate our lives to your service.

MINISTER: Break down the prejudices and barriers that divide us, and make us all one in your Son, Jesus Christ.

PEOPLE: Hear our prayer, O Lord.

MINISTER: Renew us with your Holy Spirit, which we received in our baptism, so that we might be challenged to move beyond our ruts, our apathy, and our anxieties of inadequacy.

PEOPLE: Hear our prayer, O Lord.

MINISTER: Grant that we may continuously grow in the Spirit and in the ministry that is ours as members of the priesthood of all believers, so that we may carry out our mission of service and love.

PEOPLE: Hear our prayer, O Lord.

MINISTER: Bring us at last to the joy of your eternal kingdom, so that in communion with all your saints we may evermore praise your name.

PEOPLE: Hear our prayer, O Lord.

MINISTER: Blessed Lord, draw our hearts to you, guide our minds, fill our imaginations, control our wills, for we would be wholly yours. Use us as you will, always to your glory and the welfare of your people. We pray through your Son, Jesus Christ, our Lord, who lives and reigns with you and the Holy Spirit, one God, now and forever.

PEOPLE: Amen.

Offering

Anthem

MINISTER: Break forth into exclamations of joy and gladness, you who serve the Lord.

PEOPLE: Praise the Lord! He is our God forever.

MINISTER: He made us, we belong to him.

PEOPLE: We are his sons and daughters.

MINISTER: His love for us never runs out.

PEOPLE: His care and concern for us will go on forever.

MINISTER: Then let the world see our joy.

PEOPLE: Let us lift up our voices in songs and praise and take the Good News to every nation.

MINISTER: Go, therefore, with the blessing of God almighty—the Father, the Son, and the Holy Spirit.

PEOPLE: Amen! Thanks be to God!

Recessional

Hymn

Postlude

First English Lutheran Church,
Austin, Texas,
Robert J. Karli, pastor

Litany for the Commissioning of an Adult Church School Class

MINISTER: This is a special thing we do today as we commission a new adult church school class. This is a group of adults who has a growing vision for this congregation and a clear view of their place in the church of Jesus Christ. They have insight into their own lives, and they now band themselves together so that as one they may continue to increase in their learning, their fellowship, and their service.

We now recognize these charter members of this new class. Please stand and tell us why you are here.

CLASS (stand): We come because we love the church, and we desire to serve it and the world through it. We find that we are stronger together than we are individually, and we are discovering a love for each other as we continue to work and learn. We are a class.

MINISTER: You are a part within the total life of the church universal. You are part of the living body of this congregation. Do you intend to grow in fellowship, to deepen your lives as you teach and learn, to witness to the good news of Jesus Christ as you experience it, and to worship and serve as part of the whole church universal?

CLASS: We do.

MINISTER: And do you in the congregation not represented in this class accept this class as a group of adults with their own integrity, their own life, and their own responsibility within the purposes and ideals of the church and this congregation?

PEOPLE: We do.

MINISTER: Will you support them as they continue to seek their places in the church? Will you love them as wise family, being frequent in appreciation and seldom in judgment?

PEOPLE: We will.

MINISTER: Do you now covenant together in love for the purpose of building up the body of Christ?

ALL: We do.

MINISTER: I now declare that this class is properly commissioned to grow in faith, in service, and in the building up of the church, the body of Christ. Amen.

Central Christian Church,
Granite City, Illinois,
V. Dennis Rutledge, pastor

Part **5** **Other Services**

Litany for the Blessing of a New Home

MINISTER (reads): Matthew 7:24–27

MINISTER: Happy is the family that has a home built by loyal hearts. For home is not merely a dwelling but a living fellowship. We are together in this place today to ask God's blessing on this home.

MINISTER (reads): 1 John 4:7–21

HUSBAND: We dedicate our home to love and understanding. May its joys and sorrows be shared, and the individuality of each member appreciated.

WIFE: We dedicate our home to work and leisure. May it have happiness and close fellowship, with kindness in its voices and laughter within its walls.

HUSBAND: We dedicate our home to a friendly life. May its doors open in hospitality and its windows look out with kindness.

WIFE: We dedicate our home to cooperation. May its duties be performed in love, its comforts bear witness that the work of others ministers to our needs, and its table remind us of God's bounty.

BOTH: We dedicate our home to being a part of the kingdom of God, a place for worship and Christian nurture and a threshold to life eternal.

FAMILY (prays): O God, by whom the family on earth was created and named, bestow upon our household the grace that shall keep us in the fellowship of the Christian way. Grant to each of us the heavenly guidance and control of all our labors, pleasures, and trials that shall maintain our hearts in peace and holy love with one another and with you. Graciously help and prosper us in the doing of our various duties by encouraging our willing and cheerful mind. Defend us all, by your almighty power, both from inward evil and outward harm, so that when the day is ended, it may leave us not in sorrow, strife, or shame but in true unity and thankful rest. Give us grace to deny ourselves, to take up our crosses daily, and to follow in the footsteps of Christ Jesus our Lord. Amen.

PEOPLE: O God, bless this home and those who live in it. Help them to live together in a way that your blessing may rest on them and your joy be in their hearts. Consecrate it by your own indwelling, that its light may so shine before others that they shall glorify you. Through Jesus Christ our Lord we pray. Amen.

FAMILY: We who make up this family believe that we have been united by the love of God. We desire that every plan and act, every thought and word shall be worthy of the love we have expressed, and that our inevitable disagreements may be resolved in the spirit of fairness and affection.

MEN: God, bless this family with appreciation for the house's builders and with gratitude for your leading them here to make a home.

WOMEN: Bless the doors to security and hospitality.

MEN: Bless the use of the furniture and equipment, accompanied by pleasant thoughts of all those whose work adds to comfort.

WOMEN: Bless the books as invitations to fellowship with great souls and as bearers of the truth that makes us free.

MEN: Bless the pictures as symbols of all things beautiful.

WOMEN: Bless this home to love and camaraderie, to courage and patience, to courtesy and mutual understanding, to loyalty and close fellowship.

MEN: Bless the life of this home to the service of God and all of God's children.

ALL: Bless all those who enter these doors, family and guests, with the presence, peace, and love of God.

MINISTER: Eternal God, we recognize you as the source and giver of the love that draws families together. We pray that you will be present in this

home, that your love may enrich its fellowship,
your wisdom be its guide, your truth its light, and
your peace its benediction, through Jesus Christ our
Lord we pray. Amen.

First Christian Church,
Burnet, Texas,
Robert M. Howard, pastor;

Copperas Cove Christian Church,
Copperas Cove, Texas,
Marilyn M. Howard, pastor

Litany for the Dedication of an Ethnic Social Club Building

MINISTER: In the name of the Father, and of the Son, and of the Holy Spirit,

PEOPLE: Amen.

MINISTER: To your glory and honor, O triune God,

PEOPLE: We dedicate this building.

MINISTER: That all that is good, true, and noble of the _____ culture may be brought to this place, that your people may come to know and understand your love, justice, and righteousness,

PEOPLE: We dedicate this building.

MINISTER: That the music of the soul may be expressed in song,

PEOPLE: We dedicate this building.

MINISTER: That the fellowship of people from all walks of life and all cultures may be encouraged,

PEOPLE: We dedicate this building.

MINISTER: That the celebration of the events of our lives may be shared with many,

PEOPLE: We dedicate this building.

MINISTER: That the recreation of our bodies may be accompanied by fellowship with kindred souls,

PEOPLE: We dedicate this building.

MINISTER: For being a place in this community where those interested in maintaining and nurturing the _____ culture may meet and share,

PEOPLE: We dedicate this building.

MINISTER: For the rich and ongoing history of this organization, for the numerous people who have given generously to the building program and have worked to bring it to completion, and for the times in which we live that have made it all possible,

PEOPLE: We give you thanks, O God.

MINISTER: Lord, receive now, as part of our participation in your love, justice, and righteousness, what we here offer you, and grant that we may continue in your grace in the years to come.

PEOPLE: Amen.

Austin Saenguerrunde,
Austin, Texas,
Albert W. Holck, chaplain

Litany in Recognition of a Hospital Baptism

MINISTER: We gather together in this house of God at this time to proclaim with the parents of this child that which has nurtured them in the Christian faith. To that end, these parents bring their child to be dedicated.

There are a variety of reasons why children are dedicated rather than baptized in the usual custom of our religious heritage. _____ has already received baptism because of severe illness at the time of birth. The baptism took place in the hospital. We will not rebaptize this child. We do, however, want to have an opportunity for his/her parents and this congregation to enter into a covenant regarding this faith stance.

Today we witness the fact that these parents claim the Christian faith as paramount to their living and that they desire their children to be recognized as a part of this fellowship of believers in Christ's name.

Jesus calls each of us into his presence for blessing. Mark's Gospel tells us: They were bringing children to him, that he might bless them; and the disciples rebuked them. But Jesus saw it and was indignant, and said to them, "Let the children come to me, do not hinder them; for to such belongs the kingdom of heaven. Truly I say to you, whoever does not receive the kingdom of God like a child shall not enter it." And he took them into his arms and blessed them, laying this hands on them.

Jesus also asks us to become witnesses of his Word so that all may know his way and be a part of his fellowship of faith. To this end he sends us all into the world to be living ambassadors of our faith.

I ask you now, parents and friends of _____, do you believe in Jesus Christ as our Lord and Savior, and do you desire that your child know him as Lord as well?

PEOPLE: We do.

MINISTER: Will you provide a Christian home for this child and bring him/her up in the worship and teachings of the church of Jesus Christ so that he/she may come to know him as personal Savior?

PARENTS: We will, with the help of God.

MINISTER: Dear friends of this congregation, you have heard the intentions of these parents. Will you do your part to encourage them and their child so that all may more fully find the Lord revealed to them?

PEOPLE: We will, with the help of God.

MINISTER (prays): Lord, we thank you for children. We thank you for the holy privilege of being parents.

We thank you for the gift of life, truly a holy miracle from your blessed hand. Be with this child and these parents so that all may come to know more fully the meaning of oneness in you. Amen.

This child has received baptism in the name of the Father, the Son, and the Holy Spirit. I now proceed to bless _____ and welcome him/her into the fellowship and care of Christ's church by witness of the faith of these parents and their promise to raise their child in the sight of God, and by the example and witness of this assembled fellowship of God's people. Join us, child of God, in our Christian pilgrimage.

I now present to the congregation (minister holds child for congregation to see) this child of God, the newest member of this Christian church. Let the people say amen.

PEOPLE: Let all the people say amen!

St. Peter's United Church of Christ,
Amherst, Ohio,
Joseph R. Foster, pastor

Litany for the Dedication of a Community Building and Flagstaff

MINISTER: O God of truth and grace, before whom the generations rise and pass away, we gather here to offer our thanks for all those who have gone before us and blessed us and our world with their lives and labors: patriarchs, prophets, and apostles, the wise and brave of every land and nation, and all your faithful servants.

PEOPLE: We praise and bless your name, O Lord.

MINISTER: In grateful remembrance of those of former days who shared life's journey with us and were as lamps to our feet and lights to our path,

PEOPLE: We praise and bless your name, O Lord.

MINISTER: Because you continue to inspire men and women to offer gifts in memory of loved ones, and because they serve to lift the hearts and kindle the faith of succeeding generations,

PEOPLE: We praise and bless your name, O Lord.

MINISTER: For the skill of those who designed and erected this community building and fashioned this flagstaff and flag; for the kindness and generosity of those who made them possible, for the special uses to which they are now being set apart,

PEOPLE: We praise and bless your name, O Lord.

MINISTER: In loving memory of _____ , warm friend, wise counselor, able colleague, and cherished companion,

PEOPLE: We dedicate this community building, this flagstaff, and this flag.

MINISTER: For the benefit of all who come to live here, for the inspiration of all who come to visit, and for the furtherance of a genuine sense of community and a warm feeling of belonging,

PEOPLE: We dedicate this community building, this flagstaff and flag.

ALL: Most gracious God, Father of us all, receive now from our hands these memorials, which we dedicate to your glory and the good of all your people. Bless those who have given them and those who dwell here, and bestow your favor on all who have contributed to the making of this place. Let your presence so fill this place and your spirit so dwell in the hearts of your people, that we may be led to praise you more worthily and serve you more faithfully. Through Jesus Christ our Lord we pray. Amen.

Raising of the Flag

Pledge of Allegiance

Closing Hymn

*First Congregational Church,
Harwich, Massachusetts,
Albert C. Ronander, pastor*

Litany for the Rededication of a Parsonage

MINISTER: Today it is our great privilege and pleasure to celebrate the completion of the remodeling of the parsonage and to rededicate it to the glory of God.

From Old Testament days Nehemiah reports, "So we built the wall; and all the wall was joined together to half its height. For the people had a mind to work" (Neh. 4:6).

PEOPLE: Moses said to all the congregation of the people of Israel, "This is the thing which the LORD has commanded. Take from among you an offering to the LORD; whoever is of a generous heart, let him bring the LORD's offering."

MINISTER: "And they came, everyone whose heart stirred him, and every one whose spirit moved him, and brought the LORD's offering. All who were of a willing heart . . . " (Exod. 35:4–5, 21–22).

PEOPLE: "Unless the LORD builds the house, those who build it labor in vain" (Ps. 127:1).

MINISTER: Many years ago the members of this congregation had the desire to hear the Word of God and to spread the gospel of Jesus to their families, neighbors, community, and the world. With vision and eagerness they purchased the parsonage to be a home for their pastor. And now with willing minds and generous hearts to work and give, we have repaired and renewed the parsonage for continued ministry, for our pastor's comfort and convenience, for the glory and honor of our Lord, and for this work in our lives and in the lives of those who are not yet his children.

In the New Testament we are told to use our homes to show hospitality to others.

PEOPLE: "Let brotherly love continue. Do not neglect to show hospitality to strangers, for thereby some have entertained angels unawares" (Heb. 13:1–2).

MINISTER: "Welcome one another, therefore, as Christ has welcomed you, for the glory of God" (Rom. 15:7).

PEOPLE: "And when [Lydia] was baptized, with her household, she besought us, saying 'If you have judged me to be faithful to the Lord, come to my house and stay'" (Acts 16:15).

MINISTER (prays): O blessed Father, we praise you for giving us, your people, generous hearts to give and willing hands to work so that the renovation of the parsonage might be completed. Let us not think we have now finished our work; let us rather regard this house as the sign of the ministry we are here to do, and of the gospel you have entrusted to us to share.

ALL: And now we rededicate this house, ourselves, and each of our homes to your service and to the mission of saving precious lives for your kingdom. Hear us, dear Father, in the name of Jesus. Amen.

Amana Lutheran Church,
Scandia, Kansas,
Robert E. Crofton, pastor

Additional Litanies and Dedication Services

Acolyte Robes and Stoles
Altar
Attendance Pads and Covers
Baptismal Font/Bowl
Bells
Bibles and Bible Stand
Burial of Ashes at Sea
Burning a Mortgage
Candelabra
Chalices
Chapel
Chimes
Choir Robes
Closing of a Sanctuary
Columbarium
Communion Ware
Cornerstone
Cross Lifting
Doors
Financial Pledges
Funeral Home
Funeral Pall
Ground Breaking

Hand Bells
Headstone
Home for Senior Citizens
Hospital
Hymnals
Kneeling Bench
Lectern
Merging Congregations
Movie Projector
Note Burning
Office Machines
Organ Chimes
Parking Lot
Plantings
Recognition of Adoption
Recognition of Former Pastors
Steeple and Bell
Swimming Pool
Visitation Teams
Welcome Card Pew Racks
Windows

A photocopy of any one or more of these services is available from Church Management, Inc., P. O. Box 162527, Austin, TX 78716. Please send $3.50 in check or money order (for each order selected) and a stamped business size envelope with your name and address.